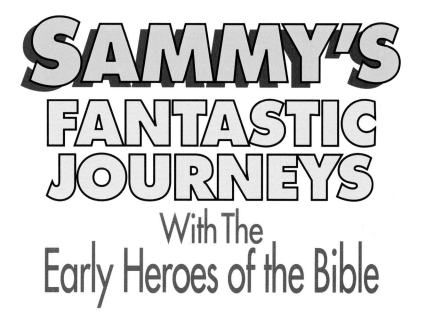

SAMMY'S FANTASTIC JOURNEYS

With The
Early Heroes of the Bible

Titles
in
A Seeking Sammy Book
series:

Sammy's Fantastic Journeys
with the
Early Heroes of the Bible

Sammy's Incredible Travels
with
Jesus and His Friends

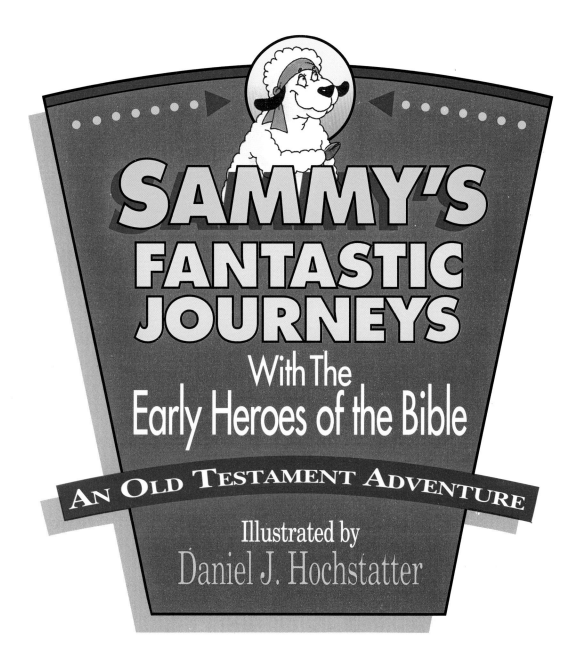

SAMMY'S FANTASTIC JOURNEYS

With The
Early Heroes of the Bible

AN OLD TESTAMENT ADVENTURE

Illustrated by
Daniel J. Hochstatter

OLIVER NELSON

A division of
THOMAS NELSON PUBLISHERS
Nashville

Published in Nashville, Tennessee, by Oliver-Nelson Books, a division of Thomas Nelson, Inc., Publishers, and distributed in Canada by Lawson Falle, Ltd., Cambridge, Ontario.

The Bible version used in this publication is THE NEW KING JAMES VERSION. Copyright © 1979, 1980, 1982, Thomas Nelson, Inc., Publishers.

Printed in the United States of America

Library of Congress Cataloging-in-Publication Data

Hochstatter, Daniel J.
    Sammy's fantastic journeys with the early heroes of the Bible / Daniel J. Hochstatter.
        p. cm. —
    Summary: A shepherd boy relates well-known Bible stories, including himself and his sheep Sammy in each one. The reader may search for the shepherd boy and Sammy in the illustrations.
        ISBN 0-8407-9161-5
        1. Bible stories, English—O.T. [1. Bible stories—O.T.]
I. Title. II. Series.
BS551.2.H58   1991
221.9'505—dc20   91-30627
                                        CIP
                                        AC

2 3 4 5 6 —97 96 95 94 93 92

SAMMY'S
FANTASTIC JOURNEYS
With the Early Heroes of the Bible

It all started because . . .

I am a shepherd boy. I spend many days and nights in the hills taking care of my sheep. Usually I am out there all alone. Sometimes I miss having someone to talk with.

One of the lambs, Sammy, stays close by me. We have become good friends. When I get really bored I like to sit and tell Sammy a story. Now I know a sheep cannot understand what I am saying, but sometimes I wonder . . .

I like Bible stories most of all. As I tell what happened in each story, I see Sammy looking off into space. He seems to be imagining how it might have been. I wonder if Sammy and I are in the pictures along with all the characters—even heroes like David, Joshua, Noah, and Daniel? I wonder what else Sammy sees in those pictures.

See if you can find Sammy and me in the pictures that follow. Join us in our adventures. And while you're at it, see how many crazy things you can find. There are some at the bottom of each page. If you get really good, try to find the ones listed on the page at the end of the book.

Find Sammy, the Shepherd, and as many of these things as you can.

 Jumping Fish

 Fish Flip

Monkey Jockey

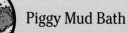 Piggy Mud Bath

IN THE GARDEN

—Genesis 1-3

God created a beautiful garden named Eden. He put Adam and Eve in the garden. They were to take care of the plants and animals and enjoy God's company. God gave Adam and Eve everything they needed. But He told them that if they ate the fruit of a certain tree, they would die.

Satan, who was very clever, tricked Eve into eating from that tree. Eve got Adam to eat from it, too.

God made Adam and Eve leave His beautiful garden.

Underwater Headstand

Fast Turtle

Find Sammy, the Shepherd, and as many of these things as you can.

 Confused Snake

 Upset Fish

 Yanked Fox

Diver

NOAH'S ARK

WET PITCH

NO CUTS PLEASE!

NOAH'S ARK

—Genesis 6-7

People on earth sinned more and more. God saw what was happening and was sorry He had ever created them. God decided to destroy everyone except Noah and his family. They were the only ones who pleased Him.

God told Noah to build a huge boat for himself, his family, and every kind of animal. Building the boat took 120 years, but Noah obeyed God.

When the boat was finished God made it rain forty days and nights. The world was so completely flooded that only Noah, his family, and the animals on the ark survived.

Squirrel Throwing Nuts

Banana Bunch Falling

Find Sammy, the Shepherd, and as many of these things as you can.

 Barber Mouse

 Snoozer

 Black Sheep

Smiling Rock

THE TOWER OF BABEL

—Genesis 11

Long ago everyone on earth spoke the same language. Many of the people lived together on a plain. They decided to build a city with a tower so tall it would reach to the sky. The people wanted to make a name for themselves. But God did not like what they were trying to do with the tower. He made everyone speak a different language.

The city became known as Babel, which means "confusion," because the people could not understand one another.

Mouse in Midair

Mouse on Scaffold

Find Sammy, the Shepherd, and as many of these things as you can.

 Bone

Mouse

Singing Sheep

 Balanced Ball

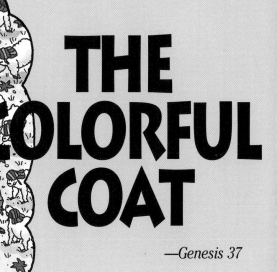

THE COLORFUL COAT

—*Genesis 37*

Jacob had twelve sons, but he loved Joseph more than the others. Jacob even made a special coat of many colors for Joseph. That made the brothers very angry, and they would not speak nicely to Joseph.

Joseph had a dream that his brothers would one day bow down to him. When he told them about it, they became even more angry with him. They decided to get rid of him.

Pizza

Black Sheep

Find Sammy, the Shepherd, and as many of these things as you can.

Very Big Basket

Strong Baby

Giant Salt Shaker

Smiling Rock

THE EXODUS

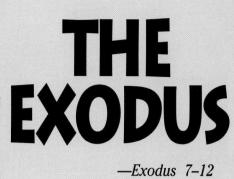

—Exodus 7–12

The Hebrew people had been slaves in Egypt for many, many years. They kept crying out to God for help. God sent Moses to tell the Egyptian king, Pharaoh, to let the Hebrew people go to another land. Not until ten terrible plagues wrecked the land, animals, and Egyptians did Pharaoh free the Hebrews. Then Moses led the six hundred thousand fighting men (add to that number all the women, children, and men who were not strong) out of Egypt.

We call this event the Exodus.

Police Officer

Singing Trio

Find Sammy, the Shepherd, and as many of these things as you can.

 Pot of Gold Coins

 Hungry Lamb

 Man Jumping Off Rock

 Baby in Diapers

THE GOLDEN CALF

—*Exodus 32*

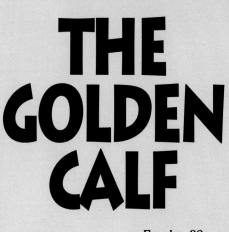

Moses left the wandering Hebrews to go up the mountain to receive orders from God. While he was gone the people became restless. They went to Aaron, Moses' brother, and insisted that he make a god to lead them.

The people gave their gold to Aaron. He melted it down and formed it into an idol that looked like a calf.

The Hebrews were bowing down and dancing before the golden calf when Moses returned.

Moses saw what they were doing and became very angry. He burned the idol and ground it into powder. Then he scattered the powder on the water and made the people drink it.

Woman Plugging Her Ears

Man Doing Handstand
on Sheep

Find Sammy, the Shepherd, and as many of these things as you can.

Snoozer

Diver

Sunbather

Big Pencil

THE BATTLE OF JERICHO

—Joshua 6

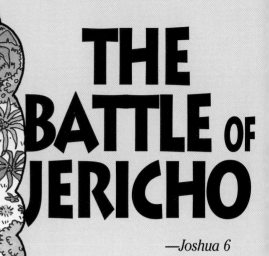

God gave Joshua special instructions to defeat the enemy at Jericho.

God told Joshua to have all his men march around the city once each day for six days. On the seventh day they were to march around the city seven times. Then the priests were to blow rams' horns, and the men were to shout. Joshua probably thought the plan was strange, but he obeyed God anyway.

God kept His word and the walls came tumbling down.

Plate of Eggs

Soldier with Sling Shot

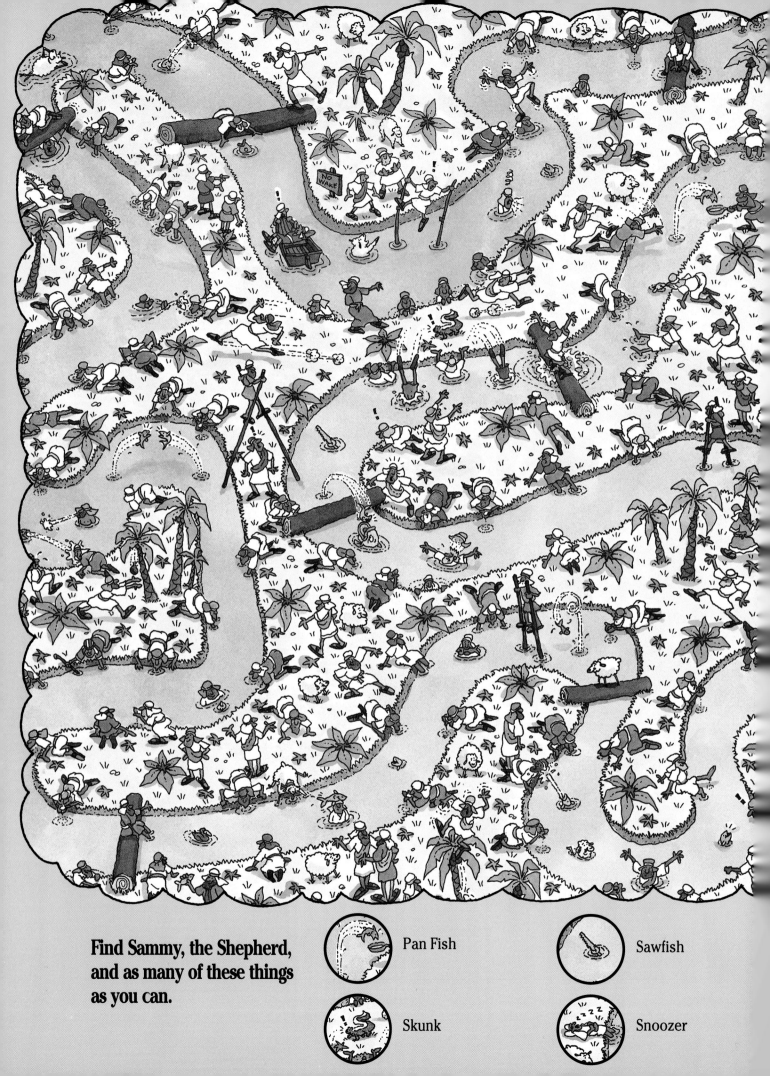

Find Sammy, the Shepherd, and as many of these things as you can.

Pan Fish

Sawfish

Skunk

Snoozer

GENERAL GIDEON

—*Judges 7*

Gideon, God's chosen leader, was preparing for battle with the enemies of the Israelites.

God said to Gideon, "You have too many men. The people might think they won the victory all by themselves. Send home all who are afraid." Gideon did as God said, but he still had ten thousand men.

God told Gideon to have all the men go to the stream. He was to send home all who got down on both knees to drink.

Only three hundred men were left. God gave them the victory over a much larger number of enemy soldiers. Everyone knew that it was God's victory and that God was with Gideon.

Midair Collision

Floating Fish

Find Sammy, the Shepherd, and as many of these things as you can.

 Cannonball Lamb

 Bird with Flag

 Yelling Lamb

 Sunbather

DAVID AND GOLIATH

—1 Samuel 17

The Philistine armies were ready for a battle with Israel's armies. The Philistines had a champion—a nine-foot-tall giant named Goliath. He stood before his armies and yelled at the Israelites, "Send your best man to fight me. If he kills me, we will be your servants. If not, you will be our servants." No one in Israel's armies would take the challenge.

David, a shepherd boy, had come near the battle lines to bring food to his brothers. He heard Goliath defying the armies of Israel, and he was outraged. David said that he would fight the giant. God had helped David before, and he knew God would help him again.

That day God used David's sling and one smooth stone to kill the mighty Goliath.

Hungry Dog Jumping

Bird in Pain

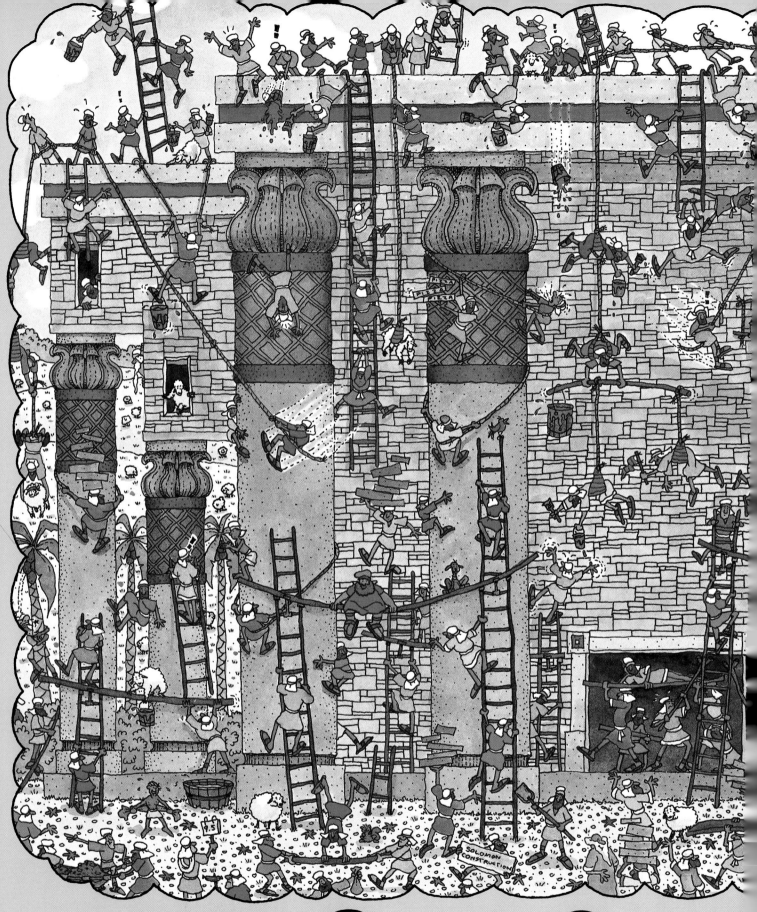

Find Sammy, the Shepherd, and as many of these things as you can.

 Diver

 Monkey

 Falling Paint Bucket

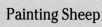 Painting Sheep

SOLOMON BUILDS THE TEMPLE

—1 Kings 5-7

King David, Solomon's father, had plans for a beautiful temple where people could worship God. God liked the idea, but He didn't want David to build the temple because he was a man of war.

So David collected building supplies for Solomon to use later. When Solomon became king, work on the temple began. In addition to stone and wood, the workers used gold and other precious materials. The temple was a magnificent and inspiring place to worship. The Lord was pleased, and He made His presence felt there.

Dog

Man with Flag

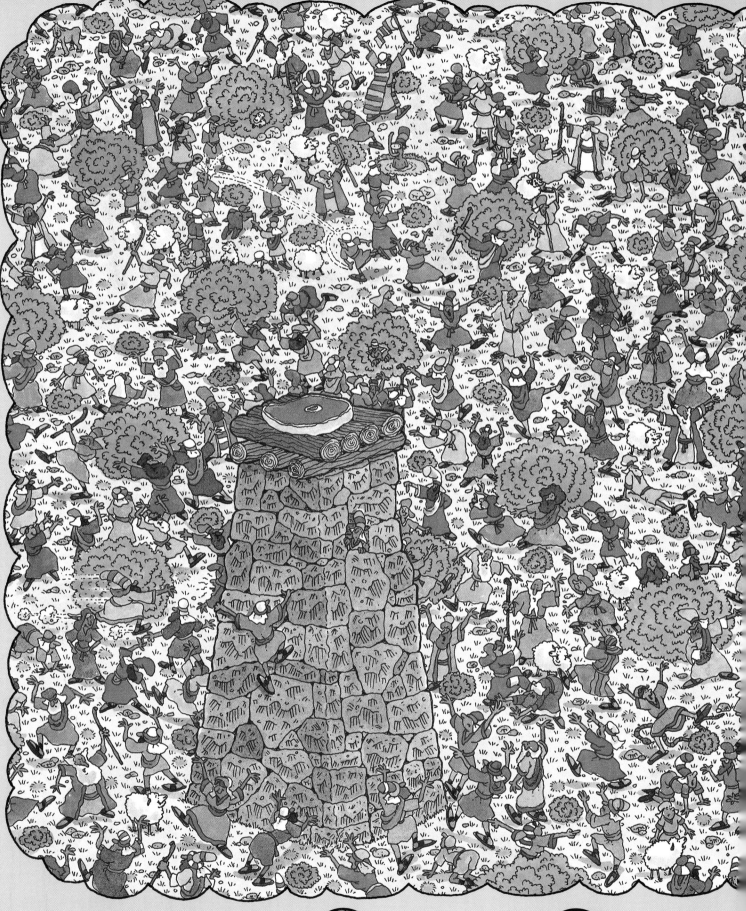

Find Sammy, the Shepherd, and as many of these things as you can.

 Picnic Basket

 Bird

Striped Flag

Swimming Hole

ELIJAH

—1 Kings 18

Elijah was a prophet of God. He challenged the prophets of Baal, a false god, to a showdown. Once and for all, he wanted to prove to the Israelites which God was real.

The prophets of Baal agreed to the test. They built their altar and then called and called and called on Baal to send down fire. Nothing happened.

Elijah built his altar, soaked the wood on it with water, and called on God to send down fire. The fire that flashed from heaven burned the wood and even the stones of the altar!

Man with Shovel

Old Man with Sunglasses

Find Sammy, the Shepherd, and as many of these things as you can.

 Baby in Diaper

 Fish in Mouth

 Man-Hole in Table

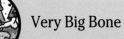 Very Big Bone

AMAZING WRITING ON THE WALL

—Daniel 5

King Belshazzar and his many banquet guests were having a wild time. Suddenly human fingers appeared and wrote on a wall. The king was scared and puzzled.

None of his wise men could explain what the writing meant, so King Belshazzar sent for Daniel. Daniel said the writing meant Belshazzar would die, and the Medes and Persians would take over his kingdom. That's exactly what happened that very night.

Bone Bearded Man

Spotted Dog

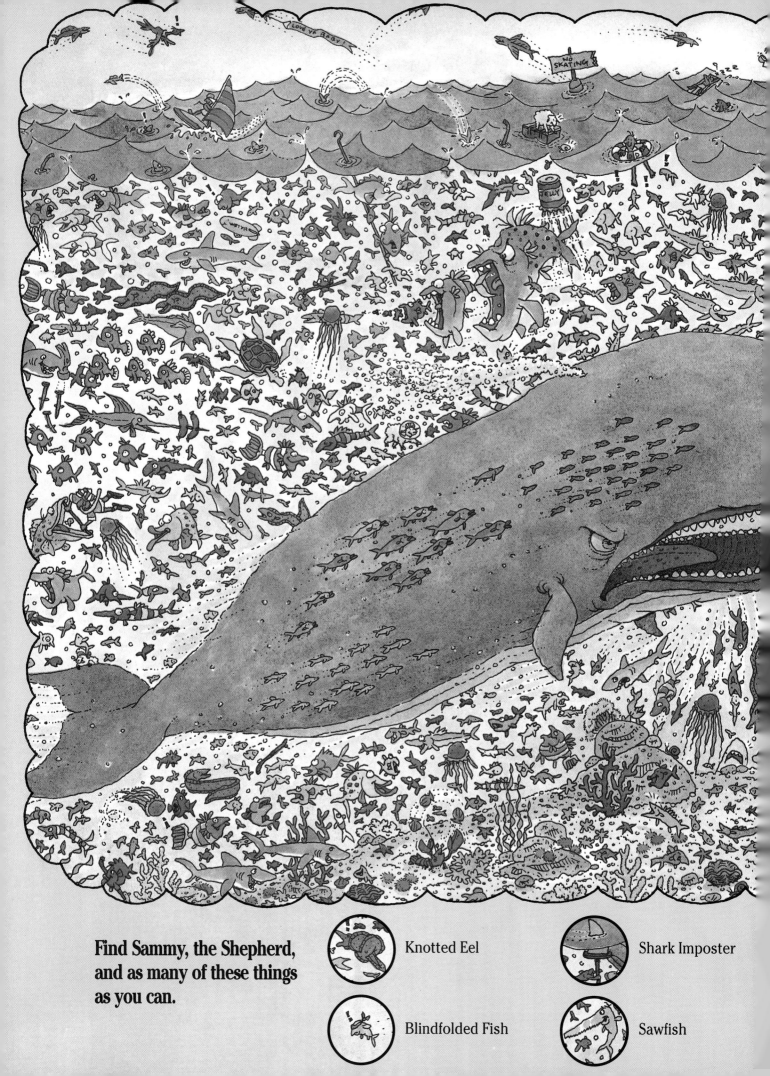

Find Sammy, the Shepherd, and as many of these things as you can.

Knotted Eel

Shark Imposter

Blindfolded Fish

Sawfish

JONAH'S LESSON

—Jonah

God told Jonah to go to Nineveh to preach against evil. Jonah did not want to, so he got on a ship going in the opposite direction.

A terrible storm blew up. Jonah knew it was storming because he had disobeyed God. He told the sailors to throw him overboard so the storm would stop. They did, and it did.

God had a huge fish swallow Jonah in one gulp. God had the fish spit him out on land three days later.

God again told Jonah to take His message to the people of Nineveh. This time Jonah obeyed.

Blimp Fish

Three Nail Fish

SEEKING SAMMY

See how many crazy things you can find

IN THE GARDEN
1. Ramming Goat
2. Fisher
3. Smiling River
4. Snoozing Bear
5. Giraffe Trio
6. Rabbits Sharing Carrot
7. Two Camels—Three Humps
8. Convict Zebra
9. Sliding Giraffe
10. Water-Fun Monkey

NOAH'S ARK
1. Bunch of Nuts
2. Ticklish Pig
3. Snoozing Giraffe
4. Butterfly Catcher
5. Juggling Seal
6. Dropped Bucket
7. Checkered Frog
8. Broken Board
9. Drying Laundry
10. White Giraffe
11. Water Hole

THE TOWER OF BABEL
1. Three-Person Elevator
2. Bowling
3. Three Upset Birds
4. Mismatched Door
5. Mouse Dropping Rock
6. Diving Board
7. Man Buried in Rock Pile
8. Skipping Ladder
9. Broken Ladder
10. Man with Chicken Leg

THE COLORFUL COAT
1. Fishing Lamb
2. Sheep Doing Cartwheel
3. Horse
4. Dog
5. Sheep with Staff in Mouth
6. Double-Hooked Staff
7. Sheep Pyramid
8. Two Dancing Sheep
9. Sheep Jumping Rope
10. Hats for Sale

THE EXODUS
1. Lemonade Stand
2. Snoozer
3. Five Person Train
4. Crowing Rooster
5. Juggler
6. Black Sheep
7. Skipping Rope
8. Woman with Two Flags
9. Choking Sheep
10. Man Carrying Three Rolls of Carpet

THE GOLDEN CALF
1. Angry Moses
2. Burned Hot Dog
3. Juggler
4. Man Standing on Another Man's Shoulders
5. Snoozer
6. Four People Holding Hands
7. Bird
8. Huge Hot Dogs
9. Human Dominoes
10. Matador

THE BATTLE OF JERICHO
1. Juggler
2. Sheep with Hat
3. Barbecue
4. Stretcher
5. Big Step
6. Cake
7. Game of Marbles
8. Two-Headed Spear
9. Pig
10. Blindfolded Soldier
11. Man Stuck in Roof

GENERAL GIDEON
1. Big Hungry Fish
2. Soldier in Tree
3. Broken Log Bridge
4. Fisher
5. Floating Lamb
6. Strong Soldier
7. Fish Juggler
8. "No Wake" Sign
9. Coconut Catcher
10. Fish on Soldier's Head
11. Two Soldiers Falling into River

DAVID AND GOLIATH
1. Fish
2. Tightrope Walker
3. Snoozer
4. Soldier Hiding in Tree
5. Sitting Horse
6. Bucking Lamb
7. Four-Person Spear
8. Lamb Riding Horse
9. Sunbathing Sheep
10. Soldier Sitting Backward on Horse

SOLOMON BUILDS THE TEMPLE
1. Pizza Delivery Person
2. Potential Collision
3. Two Men Getting Hands Stepped On
4. Dizzy Worker
5. Snoozer
6. Bird
7. Worker with Plunger
8. Very Heavy Man
9. Fisher
10. Surfer

ELIJAH
1. Snake
2. Checkered Flag
3. Dog
4. Thrown Loaf of Bread
5. Man Kissing Stone
6. Two Steaks
7. Pig
8. Juggler
9. Roasting Marshmallow
10. Snoozer
11. Man Hiding in Tree

AMAZING WRITING ON THE WALL
1. Long, Long Beard
2. Fish Juggler
3. Fisher
4. Snoozer
5. Monkey
6. Very Thirsty Fish
7. Man Slipping on Banana Peel
8. Jumping Fish
9. Dog with Bone in Mouth
10. Bone in Man's Mouth
11. Trampoline

JONAH'S LESSON
1. Mermaid
2. Clam Juggler
3. Dizzy Jellyfish
4. Six-Course Food Chain
5. Real Jellyfish
6. Snoozer
7. Smiling-Face Fish Group
8. Hammerhead Shark
9. Turtle Between Rock and Hard Place
10. Swordfish Fencing
11. Two Sea Wieners